ALL ABOUT BUTTERFLIES

The lifecycle of a Small Tortoiseshell (see also page 46). The female (far left) lays eggs on a nettle plant. After hatching, the caterpillars (centre) feed for 5–7 weeks on the leaves of the plant, before transforming into pale-coloured pupae (far right, top). Adult butterflies emerge after 2–3 weeks (far right, bottom).

ALL ABOUT
BUTTERFLIES

Matthew Oates

NEW
HOLLAND

First published in 2008 by New Holland Publishers (UK) Ltd
London • Cape Town • Sydney • Auckland

www.newhollandpublishers.com

Garfield House, 86-88 Edgware Road, London W2 2EA, United Kingdom
80 McKenzie Street, Cape Town 8001, South Africa
Unit 1, 66 Gibbes Street, Chatswood, New South Wales, Australia 2067
218 Lake Road, Northcote, Auckland, New Zealand

ISBN 978 1 84773 050 3

Senior Editor: Krystyna Mayer
Design: Fetherstonhaugh (www.fetherstonhaugh.com)
Production: Melanie Dowland
Editorial Consultant: James Parry
Editorial Direction: Rosemary Wilkinson

CONTENTS

WHAT IS A BUTTERFLY?

People like butterflies. They are fun to watch and great to study. They are a part of our summers, like visits to the seaside. They don't bite or sting, and don't do any harm – although Cabbage White caterpillars do make holes in cabbage leaves.

Butterflies are very useful – they pollinate flowers, which means that they help turn flowers into fruit. They can teach us a lot, too: because they are very sensitive to weather, they tell us how our climate is changing. Scientists are studying this carefully.

In Britain and other parts of Europe, people used to collect butterflies. But butterflies were much more common then. Today we collect pictures of butterflies by photographing them. It is a great hobby!

Butterflies are grouped into families that have many things in common.

Skippers
There are lots of Skipper butterflies in the world. The ones that live in Europe are small or even tiny, and are orange, brown or grey. Many are very hard to tell apart. Most fly very fast. Some can live in numbers together, but others live all by themselves.

Swallowtails, Festoons and Apollos
These are very smart butterflies but only one of them, the Swallowtail, lives in Britain.

Whites
The butterflies in this family are white or yellow. Some are hard to tell apart.

Blues
These are tricky to learn. In some species it is only the males that are blue, while the females are brown and look like each other.

Because it is so difficult to tell the females apart, you might like to learn to recognize the blue males first before going on to learn the females.

Coppers

There are ten Copper species in Europe. Several are very rare and only one lives in Britain. They are cousins of the Blues because they have the same wing shape.

Hairstreaks

There are twelve species of Hairstreak in Europe, five of which live in Britain. Most of them fly around bushes and trees and are very hard to see – they seem to spend a lot of time sitting around in trees doing nothing! The hairstreak is a thin line on the hind-wing underside, which usually looks like a W.

Aristocrats

This group includes many of Europe's biggest and most beautiful butterflies such as the Peacock, Red Admiral and Painted Lady. A number of them are spectacular. Some are common, while others are rare. It is easy to learn to recognize most of them, but some species are hard to see.

Fritillaries

There are nine Fritillary butterflies in Britain. Most are rare and live only in special places like nature reserves and national parks. Several are also very difficult to tell apart. Learn the easy ones first, which are also the ones you are most likely to see.

Browns

There are lots of these butterflies in Europe. Many of them are very hard to tell apart, but most of the eleven species that live in Britain are fairly easy.

FROM EGG TO BUTTERFLY

The life of a butterfly is amazing!

The Comma caterpillar mimicks bird-droppings, a means of confusing predators!

- A tiny egg is laid on a leaf.

- Inside it is a baby caterpillar (or larva).

- The egg hatches.

- The little caterpillar eats and eats and eats.

- And grows bigger and bigger.

- Changing its skin, like a snake, several times.

- Then it turns into a pupa (also called a chrysalis).

- Nothing happens for a time...

- Then the butterfly comes out.

- But with crumpled wings – which quickly take their proper shape.

- And the butterfly flies off.

- To find a mate and produce more butterflies!

- Most butterflies only live for a week or two, but a few hibernate (spend the winter asleep) and so live for nine or ten months.

The distinctive Peacock caterpilar is equipped with awesome spines that protect it from predators.

But it's more difficult than that!

1. Winter gets in the way. Most European butterflies spend the winter as little caterpillars. But some spend it as eggs, others as pupae and a few as butterflies, hibernating. Some caterpillars feed a little on mild winter days.

2. Caterpillars are fussy, so the female butterfly lays her eggs in special places – on the right plant growing in the right place. Some caterpillars may only eat the leaves of one or two types of plant.

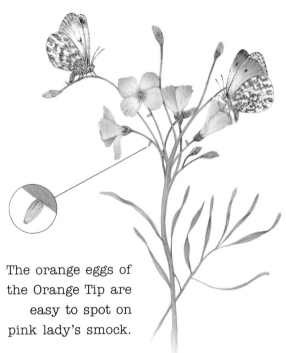

The orange eggs of the Orange Tip are easy to spot on pink lady's smock.

3. Most caterpillars of British butterflies are rather boring to look at, but a few are fantastic. The bright hairy caterpillars we sometimes find are usually moth caterpillars.

4. The plants that butterfly caterpillars eat are called food plants. Most caterpillars eat plant leaves, but a few eat buds or flowers, and Large Blue caterpillars eat ant grubs!

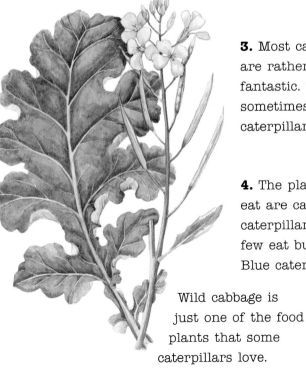

Wild cabbage is just one of the food plants that some caterpillars love.

10 THINGS YOU NEED TO KNOW ABOUT BUTTERFLIES

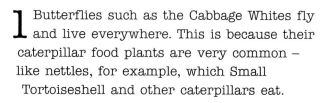

1 Butterflies such as the Cabbage Whites fly and live everywhere. This is because their caterpillar food plants are very common – like nettles, for example, which Small Tortoiseshell and other caterpillars eat.

2 Some butterflies are rare because their food plants are rare, so they only live in special places like nature reserves. They are found just in one habitat, or place that has all the things a butterfly and its caterpillars need. You will only find Adonis Blues, for example, on chalk hills because this is where their food plant grows – in this habitat they can even be common.

3 A few butterflies migrate, like the Clouded Yellow, Painted Lady and Red Admiral. They live all year in North Africa, but fly north in spring and remain in Britain for the summer. Some fly back south in the autumn.

4 Some butterfly species live in loose groups or colonies. There need to be many such groups or the butterfly will be rare. Species that live in colonies require very large areas of land like national parks.

5 Very few butterflies fly all summer long. Many only do so for four or five weeks each summer. The time when a brood of butterflies is flying is called the flight season.

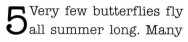

6 Some butterflies only have one brood a year, but others have two broods and some even have three. There will be more broods in the warm south than in the cool north.

7 Butterflies need to mate so that the female can go off to lay her eggs. Most female butterflies mate soon after they start to fly. They keep away from the male butterflies once the time comes for them to lay their eggs. But the males are always chasing the females about!

8 A female butterfly will lay lots of eggs – sometimes hundreds. But, like frogspawn, only a few grow up to be adult butterflies.

9 Nearly all butterflies visit flowers for a special food called nectar. A butterfly sucks nectar through its long tongue (called a proboscis), which is curled away when it is not feeding.

10 Butterflies love sunshine. Cold, wet or windy weather kills them, so they like hot summers. This is why they can tell us how our climate is changing.

11

HOW TO IDENTIFY BUTTERFLIES

1 It takes years to learn how to tell all the butterflies apart, because some are very difficult – so leave the hard ones until you've learned to recognize the easy ones!

2 The males of many butterfly species are more brightly marked than the females, and are also more easy to identify. The pictures in this book illustrate the differences between the males and females where these are very obvious.

3 The upper sides and undersides of the wings of nearly all butterflies have different markings and colours. As well as being pictured with their wings open, many of the butterflies in this

book are shown resting with their wings closed so that you can see the colours on their undersides.

4 Some butterflies – like the Brimstone, Clouded Yellow, Green Hairstreak and Grayling – only land with their wings closed. You therefore

really need to learn the undersides of these butterflies. This book tells you which butterflies only land with their wings closed.

5 It is really useful to know about the habitats of different butterflies. You will not see Adonis Blues in marshy meadows – ever! If you think you have, you've got it wrong!

6 It helps if you can learn the flight seasons of different butterflies – that is, when in the summer each species is flying. You will then know the times of year when they are most likely to be spotted.

7 In the information for each butterfly in this book the size is provided in millimetres from wing tip to wing tip. Bear in mind, however, that butterflies don't sit fully stretched out like that and may look even smaller.

8 Butterfly wing colours fade as butterflies get older: the fine coloured scales that cover the wings rub off, so old butterflies are hard to identify.

GRIZZLED SKIPPER
PYRGUS MALVAE

Male

When to see Mid-April to early June, but odd ones are seen in August in southern England if the summer is very hot.

Where to see Sheltered dry grassy places and woods.

What to look for Tiny grey butterfly with white spots. Flies close to the ground. 24 mm.

Caterpillars eat Wild strawberry and similar plants.

Did you know?
On the Continent there are 20 other butterflies that look like the Grizzled Skipper.

Male

DINGY SKIPPER
ERYNNIS TAGES

When to see May and early June. Also early August in southern England in hot summers.

Where to see Dry flowery grassland.

What to look for Looks like a brown moth, but flies like a butterfly! It is aggressive with other butterflies. 28 mm.

Caterpillars eat Mainly birdsfoot trefoil.

Did you know?
The main difference between butterflies and moths is in the shape of the antennae. Butterflies including the Dingy Skipper have hooked or clubbed antennae, while moths have feathered or thin ones.

Male

SMALL and ESSEX SKIPPERS

THYMELICUS SYLVESTRIS and T. LINEOLA

When to see Late June to early August.

Where to see Rough grassy places in England and on the Continent apart from Scotland, Ireland and Scandinavia.

What to look for Small and Essex Skippers are very hard to tell apart. The undersides of the antennae of the Essex Skipper are black, while those of the Small Skipper are orange or brown, but it is difficult to get close enough to the butterflies to spot these differences. The best time to approach them is when they are roosting in the evening or in dull weather. 26 mm.

Caterpillars eat Tall grasses. Both of these these Skippers eat the same food plants.

Male Essex Skipper

Male Small Skipper

Female Small Skipper

Did you know?

Essex Skipper caterpillars are pests in hay fields in parts of North America.

Female Small Skipper

LARGE SKIPPER
OCHLODES SYLVANUS

Did you know?
This is one of Britain's fastest-flying butterflies.

Male

When to see June to early August.

Where to see Common in woods and grassy places in most of Europe, including England and Wales. Not found in Ireland, Scotland and northern Scandinavia. One of the few butterflies regularly seen in gardens.

What to look for A large orange Skipper that flies very fast. The male has prominent black lines on each forewing. 29 mm.

Caterpillars eat Tall grasses.

SILVER-SPOTTED SKIPPER
HESPERIA COMMA

Did you know?
It is increasing nicely in south-east England and is not as rare as it was.

Male

When to see August.

Where to see In southern England, found only on chalk downs where there are lots of rabbits to keep the grass short. Not found in Ireland, Scotland and Wales. Widespread on the Continent on dry grassy hillsides.

What to look for This Skipper flies fast and very low over short grass in August. It has silver spots on its hind-wing undersides. 29 mm.

Caterpillars eat Only clumps of a short grass called sheep's fescue.

SWALLOWTAIL
PAPILIO MACHAON

When to see Mainly in June, but some can be seen in August, especially in southern Europe.

Where to see In Britain, the Swallowtail lives only in the marshes of the Norfolk Broads – it is one of the rarest British butterflies. It is widespread in continental Europe, where it lives in other habitats, breeding on a variety of different plants.

What to look for Easy! Big, black and yellow – you can usually see Swallowtails flying a long way off over the marshes. The markings of the male and female are similar. 68 mm.

Caterpillars eat In Britain they eat milk parsley, which only grows in wet places in East Anglia. On the Continent they also feed on other plants, especially wild carrot and fennel.

Male

Male

Did you know?
This is the largest British butterfly – just a little bigger than a Purple Emperor.

SCARCE SWALLOWTAIL
IPHICLIDES PODALIRIUS

Male

Did you know?

A few Scarce Swallowtails do fly over to south-east England. More may come over if the summers get hotter.

When to see There are two broods, one in spring and another in late summer.

Where to see Found in places with bushes throughout Europe, except Britain and the Scandinavian countries. Scarce Swallowtails like lavender flowers in gardens.

What to look for This is the only white Swallowtail, so it is easy to recognize. 67 mm.

Male

Caterpillars eat The leaves of blackthorn and fruit bushes.

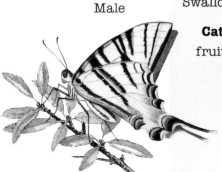

Mountain
Apollo
female

There are four species of Apollo, including the Mountain Apollo (*Parnassius apollo*), Small Apollo (*P. phoebus*) and False Apollo (*Archon apollinus*). The Clouded Apollo (*P. mnemosyne*) looks a bit like a Large White (see page 21). All four species are mountain-dwellers.

When to see The False Apollo flies in spring; the others fly in June to August.

Where to see Rough rocky slopes in mountainous regions of continental Europe. Not found in Britain.

What to look for Glorious butterflies with big red and black spots on white wings. 60 mm.

Caterpillars eat Mountain plants, especially stonecrops and house leeks.

Did you know?

Apollos are becoming rare in many places due to the decline of cows, sheep and goats as people give up farming in the mountains.

Mountain
Apollo
male

FESTOONS
ZERYNTHIA SPECIES

Southern
Festoon
male

Did you know?

Festoon butterflies fly in dry rocky places.

Southern
Festoon
female

There are three festoon butterfly species in southern Europe – the Spanish Festoon (*Zerynthia rumina*), Southern Festoon (*Z. polyxena*) and Eastern Festoon (*Z. cerisyi*). The Spanish and Southern Festoons look very similar, but the Spanish Festoon has more red spots on its forewings.

When to see Spanish and Southern Festoons fly in spring, Eastern Festoons in June.

Where to see Rough rocky hills in Spain (Spanish Festoon) and south-east Europe (Southern and Eastern Festoons).

What to look for Amazing cream, black and red butterflies. 44 mm.

Caterpillars eat Oddly named perennial plants called birthworts.

LARGE and SMALL WHITES

PIERIS BRASSICAE and P. RAPAE

Female
Large White

Did you know?

Large and Small Whites are probably better known as Cabbage Whites due to their obvious preference for cabbages. They are very successful – they were introduced into the United States from Europe in the 1860s and have since become very common there.

The Large White (55 mm) and the Small White (45 mm) are very similar. Usually the Large White is much bigger, but you get some small Large Whites and some large Small Whites.

When to see Both species fly from April to late October. You see most of them in August.

Where to see They can be found everywhere, but like gardens best – especially those with cabbages!

What to look for Both species have pale yellow on the hind-wing undersides and black tips to the front wings. Large White females in particular have more black on the front wings.

Caterpillars eat Many wild and garden plants from the cabbage family.

Female Small White

GREEN-VEINED WHITE
PIERIS NAPI

When to see Two broods: in April and May, and again in July and August.

Where to see Found throughout Britain and continental Europe. Woods and damp areas are particularly good places to see it.

What to look for There are thick grey-green veins on the yellowy wing undersides – but you have to get close to see these. Although this is a common white butterfly, it is not easy to tell it apart from the Small White (see page 21). 43 mm.

Caterpillars eat Many different garden and wild plants, especially lady's smock (like the Orange Tip on the opposite page). Although Green-veined Whites look similar to Cabbage Whites, they don't eat cabbages.

Female

Female

Did you know?
On hot days these butterflies drink from muddy puddles.

ORANGE TIP
ANTHOCHARIS CARDAMINES

Male

When to see From early April to mid-June.

Where to see Best in woods, valleys, lanes and gardens, and around ponds. Common in England and Wales, but very local in Scotland. Widespread on the Continent.

What to look for Male Orange Tips are easy to spot – this is the only white butterfly in Britain with bright orange wing tips. But the females look like small Cabbage Whites (see page 21) or Green-veined Whites (see opposite), and it is very difficult to tell them apart. 42 mm.

Caterpillars eat Mainly lady's smock and garlic mustard. They also like some garden plants, such as sweet rocket.

Did you know?
The males' bright orange wing tips act as a warning to predators. They do not taste very good because they contain bitter mustard oils from the food plants they ate at the caterpillar stage.

Male

BRIMSTONE
GONEPTERYX RHAMNI

Male

Female

When to see They fly in spring and again in July and August. Then they spend the winter hiding in ivy or brambles, looking just like leaves.

Where to see Woods, marshes and downs in England and Wales. Not found in Scotland. Rare in Ireland and northern Scandinavia.

What to look for The wings of the male Brimstone are the colour of butter. This is where the name 'butterfly' comes from! But the female is white and gets lost among the Cabbage Whites. These butterflies settle only with their wings closed. 57 mm.

Caterpillars eat Leaves of a bush called buckthorn.

Did you know?
If your first butterfly of the year is a Brimstone you will have a happy summer. It is a good sign.

CLOUDED YELLOW
COLIAS CROCEUS

When to see In Britain, mainly from early June to October, but most are seen in August and September.

Where to see Mainly in southern continental Europe, but it comes to southern Britain in hot summers. In some years large numbers reach Britain and northern parts of the Continent. It likes sunny slopes and clover fields.

What to look for A black and gold butterfly flying fast along the south slopes of hills. In the female the black wing edges are broken by ragged yellow spots. Clouded Yellows only settle with their wings closed. 47 mm.

Caterpillars eat Mainly birdsfoot trefoil and clovers, but only in very short grass.

Male

Did you know?

Clouded Yellow caterpillars are now living through the English winter on the south coast, probably because of climate change.

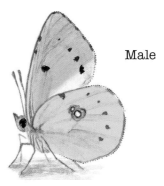
Male

25

BLACK-VEINED WHITE

APORIA CRATAEGI

Did you know?

The caterpillars of this butterfly can be a pest in orchards in southern Europe.

When to see Mainly June.

Where to see The Black-veined White was once common in southern England, but has been extinct in Britain for about 100 years. The reasons for its decline are not fully known – its food plants are plentiful in Britain. On the Continent it is found in orchards and on bushy hills.

What to look for A big white butterfly with distinctive black lines. Often roosts communally. 58 mm.

Caterpillars eat Leaves of fruit trees and blackthorn.

Male

Can sometimes be seen clustering at wet mud patches.

LARGE BLUE
GLAUCOPSYCHE ARION

Male

When to see June.

Where to see Grassy hillsides. In England, found only on a few nature reserves in the south-west. Less rare on the Continent, but always very hard to find.

What to look for It is royal blue in colour and is the largest of the Blue butterflies. Unlike many other Blues, it doesn't have orange spots on its undersides. The female's undersides are heavily spotted with black. 36 mm.

Caterpillars eat At first, wild thyme, but they then go to live, cuckoo-like, in ants' nests, where they eat ant grubs for a long time. They pupate in the ants' nests, and the butterflies then have to crawl out up the ant tunnels.

Female

Female

Did you know?

The Large Blue became extinct in England in 1979, but was reintroduced by conservationists from Sweden. It is doing well in the West Country.

SMALL BLUE
CUPIDO MINIMUS

Male

When to see May and June, and again a few in late July and early August.

Where to see Dry grassy hills on chalk and limestone, and some places by the sea. Local in Britain and in nearly all other European countries.

What to look for The smallest European butterfly. A tiny dark blue species with no orange spots. 21 mm.

Caterpillars eat Kidney vetch flowers.

Did you know?
Like many butterflies it has two broods in southern Europe but only one proper brood in the north.

LONG-TAILED BLUE
LAMPIDES BOETICUS

Did you know?
As the climate warms up, it may come to live in Britain and other parts of northern Europe.

When to see May to October, but best in August and September.

Where to see Fairly common in southern Europe, but migrates further north, occasionally reaching southern Britain. Likes rough flowery places and gardens.

What to look for A grey-blue butterfly with long tails. Flies like a Hairstreak – it flits. 32 mm.

Caterpillars eat Flowers and seedpods of wild and garden pea plants.

Male

HOLLY BLUE
CELASTRINA ARGIOLUS

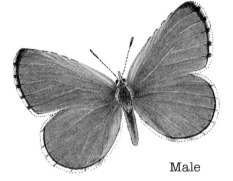

Male

When to see Two broods: April and May, and another in July and August.

Where to see Britain and other parts of Europe, except Scotland. It likes towns and gardens, woods and hedges.

What to look for A bright blue butterfly flying around shrubs and bushes. There are no orange spots on the wing undersides, as there are in many Blues, just little black dots. 32 mm.

Caterpillars eat Holly berries in spring, ivy berries in late summer.

Female

Did you know?

In some years Holly Blues are common and in others they are rare. In the years when they are rare the caterpillars get eaten by a species of small wasp.

Female

COMMON BLUE
POLYOMMATUS ICARUS

Did you know?
This is the most common Blue butterfly in Europe.

When to see May to September in two broods (three in southern Europe, but only one in Scotland).

Where to see Everywhere in dry grassy places with flowers. It even breeds in old lawns.

What to look for The males are always brilliant lilac-blue with orange spots on the undersides. The females vary in colour: they may be blue with some brown, but are sometimes only brown, and a few are dark blue. 29 mm.

Caterpillars eat Birdsfoot trefoil and clovers in short grass only.

Male

Female

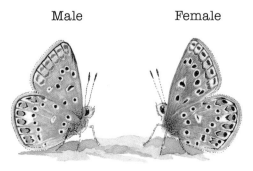

Male   Female

ADONIS BLUE
POLYOMMATUS BELLARGUS

When to see June and again in August and September.

Where to see Nature reserves on dry chalky hills in southern England. Widespread in southern and central Europe.

What to look for Brilliant electric-blue males – brighter than any other Blues. The females are deep brown and similar to female Chalkhill Blues (see page 32). 33 mm.

Caterpillars eat Horseshoe vetch – the same as the Chalkhill Blue.

Male

Female

Did you know?

The caterpillars of most Blue butterflies – and especially those of the Adonis Blue – produce a milky juice that ants love.

Male   Female

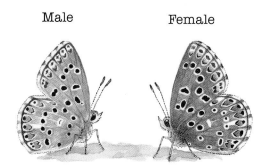

CHALKHILL BLUE

POLYOMMATUS CORIDON

Male

When to see July and August.

Where to see Dry chalky hills in southern England and central Europe. Lives in isolated colonies that can sometimes be very large – numbering as many as 20,000 or more butterflies!

What to look for The males are milky blue and look very pale when flying in bright sunlight. The females are chocolate brown. This species is larger than any other Blue butterfly in Britain apart from the Large Blue. 34 mm.

Caterpillars eat Horseshoe vetch only.

Did you know?

Sometimes there are so many Chalkhill Blues close together that you have to avoid treading on them!

Female

Male

SILVER-STUDDED BLUE
PLEBEIUS ARGUS

When to see June and July in Britain and other parts of northern Europe. Spring and late summer broods in southern Europe.

Where to see Heaths, sand dunes and some dry limestone hills. Local in England and Wales, and in most of continental Europe. Not found in Ireland or Scotland.

What to look for Very small, bright blue males. The females are brown. 25 mm.

Caterpillars eat Heathers and sometimes birdsfoot trefoil. Most colonies in England and Wales are found on sandy heaths, where there is a lot of heather.

Male

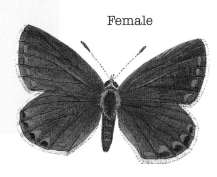

Female

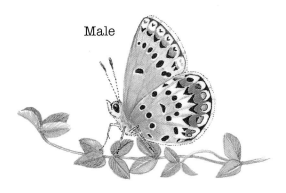

Male

Did you know?
The Silver-studded Blue doesn't have silver studs, but lead-coloured spots on its hind-wing undersides.

BROWN and NORTHERN BROWN ARGUS

PLEBEIUS AGESTIS and P. ARTAXERXES

When to see Brown Argus: May and June, and again in August. Northern Brown Argus: July.

Where to see Grassy hills and sometimes in other places too. Found in all of Europe except Ireland.

What to look for Very small brown butterflies with bright orange spots on the wing edges. The female often has bolder markings than the male. The two species are very similar, but the Northern Brown Argus usually has a small white spot on each forewing. 26 mm.

Caterpillars eat Common rockrose and sometimes cranesbills.

Did you know?

The Brown Argus and Northern Brown Argus not only look similar to each other, but also look like many female Blues. The males are aggressive, attacking other butterflies.

Male Brown Argus

Male Northern Brown Argus

Female Brown Argus

Female Brown Argus

SMALL COPPER

LYCAENA PHLAEAS

When to see April to November in three broods; best in August.

Where to see Meadows, heaths, sand dunes, dry grassy places and wasteland everywhere. Found throughout Europe.

What to look for The smallest and most common Copper. It has bright orange and brown wings. 30 mm.

Caterpillars eat Sorrels and docks.

Male

Did you know?

Sometimes there are little blue spots in the copper on the hind-wing upper sides. Look out for them!

Male

LARGE COPPER

LYCAENA DISPAR

This large and fiery butterfly is the largest Copper butterfly. In Britain it died out in the 1850s, when the marshes in which it lived were drained. It is now found mainly in central and eastern Europe, but is becoming rare in some countries. The caterpillars eat docks in very wet places. 40 mm.

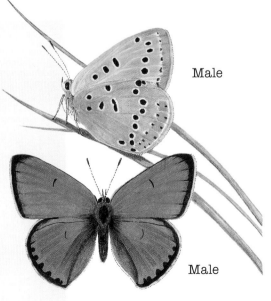

Male

Male

GREEN HAIRSTREAK
CALLOPHRYS RUBI

When to see April to mid-June in Britain.
Some can be seen in July and August in
southern Europe.

Where to see In every European country,
on heaths, downs, hillsides, moors and cliffs,
and in sand dunes, bogs and woods. It can
usually be seen around bushes, but it is
not common.

What to look for Tiny butterfly that looks brown
in the air but settles with closed wings to
show bright green undersides. 26 mm.

Caterpillars eat Both the buds and flowers
of many different plants, especially
common rockrose, birdsfoot trefoil, gorse
and bilberry.

Male

Female

Did you know?

Green Hairstreak males fight
each other a lot!

Male   Female

PURPLE HAIRSTREAK
NEOZEPHYRUS QUERCUS

Male

When to see July and August.

Where to see In and around oak woods in all European countries except northern Scotland and northern Scandinavia. These butterflies live in colonies, although this is not obvious because they spend most of the time in tree-tops.

What to look for Purple on the upper sides of the wings. The female is much less purple than the male. The undersides are grey. 37 mm.

Caterpillars eat Oak buds and leaves.

Female

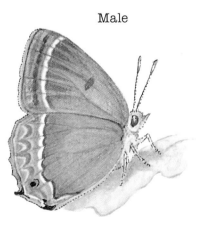

Male

Did you know?
Purple Hairstreaks fly in the evening. Look at oak trees in the sun in early evening, between 6 and 7 p.m. in July, and you may see lots of grey-looking butterflies dancing in circles together over the leaves. These will be Purple Hairstreaks.

PURPLE EMPEROR
APATURA IRIS

Male   Female

When to see Late June to early August. Most are seen in mid-July.

Where to see This huge butterfly lives high up in the tops of trees in forests and large woods in southern England and central Europe.

What to look for The Purple Emperor is rare and is one of the most difficult butterflies to see because it does not visit flowers. On some mornings male Purple Emperors fly down and settle on sunny paths in woods, to suck juices from things we consider nasty, like dog pooh! 70 mm.

Caterpillars eat The eggs are laid high up in sallow trees (pussy willow bushes). The little caterpillar spends the winter there, then feeds up quickly during May and grows as big as your middle finger. It pupates under a leaf.

Did you know?

In the afternoons the males fight and chase each other about over special trees called 'Master Trees'. These battles are amazing to watch. To find a 'Master Tree' is the biggest thrill there is in butterfly watching! The females are shy and spend a lot of time seemingly doing nothing high in the trees.

Male

TWO-TAILED PASHA

CHARAXES JASIUS

When to see Two broods, in spring and late summer.

Where to see Occurs only near or in the Mediterranean region. Not found in Britain.

What to look for A brown giant with two tails. The magnificent Two-tailed Pasha is the largest European butterfly. It is attracted to tree sap, fruit and even carrion. It flies very fast and the males defend their territory against all comers. 75 mm.

Caterpillars eat Leaves of the strawberry tree, which only grows in gardens and parks in Britain but is common near the Mediterranean.

Male

Did you know?

It is fast flying over trees on steep slopes, and very difficult to get near – it's even more difficult to see than the Purple Emperor. Males can attack you if you enter their territory!

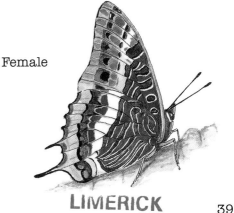

Female

WHITE ADMIRAL
LIMENITIS CAMILLA

When to see White Admirals fly from mid-June to late July. After hot summers a few more fly during September and October.

Where to see Lives in shady woods in southern England and on most of the Continent.

What to look for These lovely black and white butterflies are one of the best species to watch, as they flit and glide gracefully in and out of bushes along woodland paths. They like to feed on bramble flowers, and you can sometimes get close to them there. 56 mm.

Caterpillars eat Honeysuckle leaves, but only on plants hanging from bushes in shade under trees.

Male

Did you know?

In hot summers a few White Admirals do not have the white bands on their wings. These 'Black Admirals' are very rare.

Male

VANESSA CARDUI

Male

When to see Can be seen all through the year but is most common in summer, especially in August.

Where to see Anywhere with lots of flowers, including gardens. Sometimes you see them on the tops of high hills.

What to look for This is the only big pink and grey butterfly you will see. It can fly very fast and visits flowers a lot. 54 mm.

Caterpillars eat Thistles.

Did you know?

Painted Ladies breed mainly in Africa and around the Mediterranean, but each summer they fly north and lay their eggs and breed there. These new butterflies often fly south in autumn. In some summers there are lots of Painted Ladies in northern Europe.

Male

RED ADMIRAL
VANESSA ATALANTA

Male

When to see At any time of the year, even on sunny days in winter. Most Red Admirals are seen between July and October.

Where to see Anywhere, but especially in gardens and woods, and near the sea.

What to look for This is the only big black, white and red butterfly. You can't get it wrong! 56 mm.

Caterpillars eat Nettle leaves. They make a little tent out of a leaf to live in. Sometimes the tents are easy to find, but spiders and other caterpillars also make them and often you just find a spider inside. Look anyway, but mind the nettle stings!

Male

Did you know?
Like Peacock butterflies, some Red Admirals hibernate inside houses during winter, emerging on warm March and April days.

CAMBERWELL BEAUTY

NYMPHALIS ANTIOPA

When to see Late June to August and again in early spring after hibernation.

Where to see Woods and places with lots of trees. It is found in most European countries, but is only a very rare visitor to Britain.

What to look for Easy! A spectacular big black butterfly with yellow wing edges. The dark underwings provide camouflage when it is hibernating in hollow trees. 62 mm.

Caterpillars eat Sallow and birch leaves.

Male

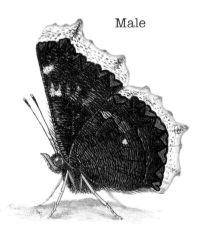

Male

Did you know?

The butterfly gets its name because the first one ever seen in Britain was caught in Camberwell in London!

PEACOCK
IANACHIS IO

Did you know?
The 'eye' markings on the upper wings are there to warn away predators. The Peacock can also produce a hissing noise by rubbing its wings together!

When to see Can be seen in any month apart from June. Peacocks emerge in July, feed on flowers and then hibernate from late August, flying on warm autumn or winter days, and then again in spring.

Where to see Lots of places, especially in towns and gardens, but rare in Scotland and not found in northern Scandinavia.

What to look for A dark red butterfly with large peacock eyes on all wings. The markings of both sexes are similar. The dark undersides look like bark, making it almost invisible when it hibernates in hollow trees and in garden sheds. 56 mm.

Caterpillars eat Stinging nettles in sunny places.

Male

Male

MAP BUTTERFLY
ARASCHNIA LEVANA

When to see There are two broods, one in spring and the other in late summer.

Where to see Woods and open places with trees in most of Europe, where it is common, but not in the north or far south. Not found in Britain.

What to look for Tricky! The two broods look very different – the spring butterflies look like small Fritillaries or Wall Browns (see page 57), but the late summer butterflies look like tiny White Admirals (see page 40). The Map Butterfly's name comes from the intricate map-like markings on its wings. 34 mm.

Caterpillars eat Nettles.

Did you know?

This little butterfly does not live in Britain – yet. It may come to live here soon because of climate change. It has recently spread all through Holland.

Spring
generation
male

Summer
generation
male

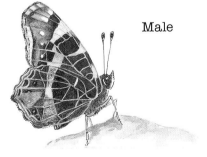

Male

SMALL TORTOISESHELL
AGLAIS URTICAE

Male

When to see Small Tortoiseshells spend the winter as butterflies and mate in spring. New butterflies fly in late June and July, and more butterflies come out in August. So you can see them easily from February to October, but they are rare in May.

Where to see Common everywhere in Europe, including in towns. It may hibernate in houses and outhouses – don't try to 'rescue' one if you see it indoors by releasing it outside in freezing weather! Put it in a shed where there is no central heating.

What to look for Orange-red butterfly with dark blue wing edges. 48 mm.

Caterpillars eat Nettles.

Did you know?

The caterpillars live together on nettles in sunny places – you can find lots of them hiding in webs that keep birds off (see also page 2). It is fun to keep a few caterpillars – but don't take too many as they are always hungry and need lots of stinging nettles.

Male

LARGE TORTOISESHELL

NYMPHALIS POLYCHLOROS

When to see February and March, and then again in July and early August. Large Tortoiseshells hibernate.

Where to see Nearly extinct in Britain and local and declining on the Continent. Found in and around woods, valleys, towns, orchards and gardens.

What to look for Huge tawny tortoiseshell, much bigger and less red than the Small Tortoiseshell. 58 mm.

Caterpillars eat Leaves of different trees.

Male

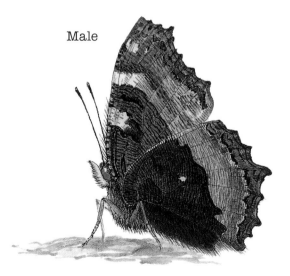

Male

Did you know?

The Large Tortoiseshell used to be widespread and sometimes common in England but has almost disappeared. We don't know why. The good news is that it may be starting to recolonize England. Perhaps it's trying to come home!

COMMA
POLYGONIA C-ALBUM

Male

Male

Did you know?
The caterpillar is weird –
most of it is brown but
the back half is white!
You can find it on the
tips of nettle plants.

When to see In spring, and then from late June
through to autumn. The Comma is a butterfly that
hibernates.

Where to see Woods, valleys and gardens, but
you never see many of them. Lives in nearly
all European countries.

What to look for The Comma is the only butterfly in Europe with very
jagged wings. Its shape and pattern make it resemble a dead leaf, and act as
great camouflage. 52 mm.

Caterpillars eat Nettles and some tree leaves, especially those of elm.

QUEEN OF SPAIN FRITILLARY
ISSORIA LATHONIA

Male

Male

Did you know?

This butterfly may colonize Britain if the climate gets warmer.

When to see Spring and especially late summer. Two broods.

Where to see Very rare migrant to Britain, but widespread in continental Europe. Found on sand dunes, sandy heaths and dry flowery meadows.

What to look for Middle-sized Fritillary with large silver patterns on the back-wing undersides. It flies like a Wall Brown (see page 57). 44 mm.

Caterpillars eat Pansies and violets.

SILVER-WASHED FRITILLARY
ARGYNNIS PAPHIA

Did you know?

The eggs are laid on tree trunks and the little caterpillars somehow manage to get to the violets – their food plant – that grow on the ground.

When to see Late June to late August; best in mid-July.

Where to see In large woods, especially of oak, in England, Wales, Ireland and all of continental Europe apart from the far north and deep south.

What to look for A friendly orange giant that loves flowers, especially brambles and thistles. The males and females look different from each other. The males are bright orange with pointed front wings. The females are less bright and have more black spots. A few females (called Valezina females) are almost green. 60 mm.

Caterpillars eat Violets growing under trees, especially oaks.

Female

Male

Male

DARK GREEN FRITILLARY

ARGYNNIS AGLAJA

When to see Late June to late August; best in July.

Where to see Found throughout Europe, on hills, sand dunes, sea cliffs and downs, and in open places in woods.

What to look for A very large Fritillary with dark green patches on the hind-wing undersides. The orange colour of the female is paler than that of the male. It is hard to tell the Dark Green Fritillary from the much rarer High Brown Fritillary. Only the Silver-washed Fritillary (shown opposite) and Cardinal (on the Continent) are bigger. 58 mm.

Caterpillars eat Violet leaves in rough grass.

Male

Did you know?

Dark Green Fritillaries are very strong flyers. They can be seen battling in wind on the tops of hills, and visiting thistle flowers.

Male

PEARL-BORDERED FRITILLARY
BOLORIA EUPHROSYNE

Did you know?
This butterfly is becoming very rare in Britain, although it was once quite common.

When to see May and early June.

Where to see In woods and on rough bracken hills throughout Europe except the far south. Rare in Ireland and also now rare in Britain.

What to look for Small Fritillary with light gold patches and silver pearls along the edges of the hind-wing undersides. 40 mm.

Caterpillars eat Violets in warm places.

Male

Male

Male

Male

SMALL PEARL-BORDERED FRITILLARY
BOLORIA SELENE

It is difficult to tell the difference between the two Fritillary species on this page. The Small Pearl-bordered Fritillary's hind-wing undersides have silver pearls, like those of the Pearl-bordered Fritillary, but they also have deep brown patches instead of gold markings. The female's upper sides have very pale pearls along the edges. Small Pearl-bordered Fritillaries are found in most of Europe, and can be seen in late May to late June. 38 mm.

Male

MARSH FRITILLARY

EUPHYDRYAS AURINIA

When to see Late May and June.

Where to see Marshy meadows, bogs and sometimes dry hills throughout Europe except for the far north. Rare in Britain, where it is found mostly on nature reserves.

What to look for A bright orange, cream and black butterfly. The females are often larger than the males. 37 mm.

Caterpillars eat Mainly devil's bit scabious.

Male

Female

Did you know?

The black caterpillars of the Marsh Fritillary live together in huge groups. Sometimes there are millions of them.

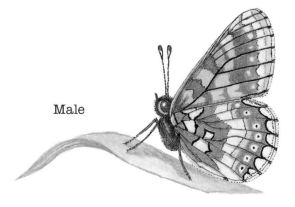

Male

GLANVILLE FRITILLARY
MELITAEA CINXIA

Did you know?
The butterfly is named after Lady Eleanor Glanville, who collected butterflies in the 1700s. People thought she was mad!

Male

When to see June.

Where to see In Britain only on the Isle of Wight, but more common on dry hillsides on the Continent.

What to look for Easy to spot on the Isle of Wight, but more difficult on the Continent as there are some similar species in a few places. 38 mm.

Caterpillars eat Plantain leaves on bare ground.

HEATH FRITILLARY
MELITAEA ATHALIA

Did you know?
Twenty-five years ago the Heath Fritillary was nearly extinct in England, but it has been saved.

Male

When to see June in England. It has 2–3 broods on the Continent.

Where to see Very rare in England – found in some woods in south-east and south-west, and on Exmoor. Common on Continent, in woods, rough fields and flowery places.

What to look for Like the Glanville Fritillary (see above), but darker. Looks black when flying. 38 mm.

Caterpillars eat Mainly common cow-wheat in England.

DUKE OF BURGUNDY

HAMEARIS LUCINA

When to see In Britain, late April and May. It has two broods in southern Europe, one in spring and the other in August.

Where to see Downs and some woods in England, and rough low hills in central Europe. It is rather rare in England.

What to look for A tiny dark brown and orange butterfly. The females have three pairs of legs, but the males have only two pairs. This butterfly lives in colonies. It is becoming rare in Britain due to changes in its habitat. 28 mm.

Caterpillars eat Cowslip and primrose.

Male

Female

Did you know?

The Duke of Burgundy is often grouped with the Fritillaries, but it is actually the only European member of an exotic tropical butterfly family called the Metalmarks!

Female

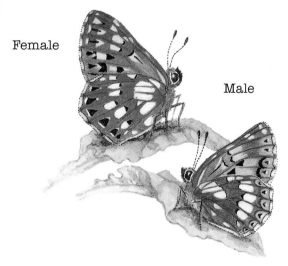

Male

SPECKLED WOOD
PARARGE AEGERIA

Did you know?

Speckled Woods spend the winter as small
or large caterpillars, which means that
the butterflies come out at
different times.

Male

Female

When to see March to
November; best in
August and September.
It has lots of broods in
the year.

Where to see Near trees and
bushes, in all of Europe apart from
northern Scandinavia. It is increasing in
Britain, especially in the north.

What to look for In Britain and other parts of
northern Europe, a dark brown butterfly with big
pale yellow spots. In southern Europe the spots
are larger and orange-brown, so the butterfly
looks like a Wall Brown (see opposite). However,
it usually flies in shady places where Wall
Browns don't go. 37 mm.

Caterpillars eat Grasses under trees.

WALL BROWN
LASIOMMATA MEGERA

When to see Late April to October in three broods.

Where to see Sunny, dry grassy places with bare ground. Not found in Scotland or Scandinavia. In England and Wales most often seen near the sea.

What to look for Orange and brown colour. 38 mm.

Caterpillars eat Grasses on sunny banks.

Did you know?
The eggs are like little pearls. They are usually laid on grass roots in the roofs of rabbit holes and along tractor ruts.

Male

MEADOW BROWN
MANIOLA JURTINA

When to see June to October, and especially July and August.

Where to see In grassy places everywhere in Britain and on the Continent, except on high mountains.

What to look for Brown with a white-eyed black spot on each front wing. The female has an orange splash on each front wing. 42 mm.

Caterpillars eat Grasses.

Female

Did you know?
This is one of Britain's most common butterflies.

GATEKEEPER
PYRONIA TITHONUS

Did you know?
The Gatekeeper is also called the Hedge Brown.

Male

When to see July and August.

Where to see Hedges and dry grassy places near trees and bushes. Not found in Scotland or Scandinavia, but quite common in southern England and most other parts of Europe.

What to look for Smaller and more orange than the Meadow Brown (see page 57). It has two white spots in the dark eye on each wing. 35 mm.

Caterpillars eat Dry grasses under bushes.

SMALL HEATH
COENONYMPHA PAMPHILUS

Did you know?
This is one of Britain's most common butterflies, yet we don't know much about what it really needs or likes.

Male

When to see May through to September. Best in June and August.

Where to see Dry grassy places all over Europe, even high in mountains. In England, most common on chalk downs.

What to look for Small butterfly with orange upper sides and grey undersides. Only settles with wings closed. 30 mm.

Caterpillars eat Small grasses.

MARBLED WHITE

MELANARGIA GALATHEA

When to see Mid-June to early August.

Where to see Grassy places on hills in southern England and Wales, and in central and southern Europe.

What to look for In Britain, the Marbled White is very easy to recognize because it is the only patchy black and white butterfly. It's more difficult to identify in Spain, where there are three other Marbled Whites that look like it. Both the male and the female have similar upper wings, but the female has a marked yellow tinge on the underwings. 45 mm.

Caterpillars eat Grasses in dry places.

Male

Did you know?

Marbled Whites now live in many parts of northern England and are heading for Scotland.

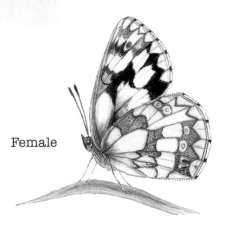

Female

RINGLET
APHANTOPUS HYPERANTUS

When to see June and July.

Where to see Rough grassy places, especially near woods. Quite common in England and Wales, but local in Scotland. In continental Europe, not found in the far north or in southern Spain.

What to look for Easy – the only nearly black butterfly with little cream rings! The female is slightly paler than the male. 40 mm.

Caterpillars eat Tall grasses.

Male

Did you know?
Ringlets will fly even in very dull weather, when other butterflies are asleep.

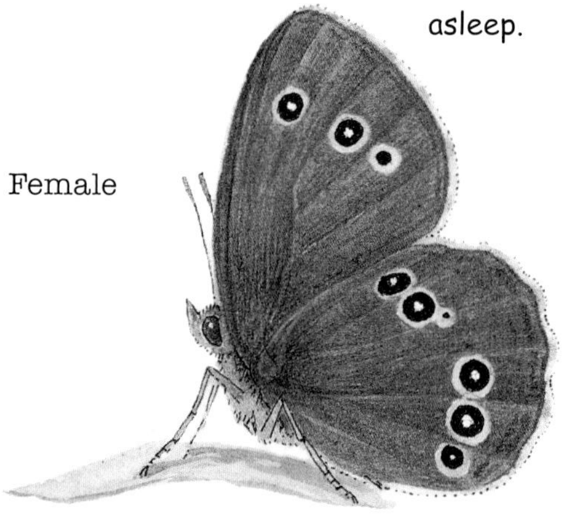

Female

When to see August.

Where to see Grassy places on hills and mountains in Scotland (and two places in northern England), and in central and eastern Europe.

What to look for Dark brown butterfly with brick-red eye-spots. The female is slightly lighter than the male. The Scotch Argus only flies when the sun is shining. At other times it hides in vegetation. 40 mm.

Caterpillars eat Rough grasses.

Male

Did you know?

There are 20 other butterflies on the Continent that look like the Scotch Argus. They live mainly in the mountains, and are rare and very hard to tell apart.

Male

GRAYLING
HIPPARCHIA SEMELE

Did you know?

Graylings often land on tree trunks and if
you stand still they may
land on your
trousers!

Female

Female

When to see July to September.

Where to see Dry, rocky or sandy
places, in all of Europe except
northern Scandinavia. In Britain,
found mostly near the sea.

What to look for Grey and orange butterfly that
only lands with its wings closed and is very
hard to spot. This is because it usually lands
on bare ground, against which it is perfectly
camouflaged. The female's markings are
brighter and bolder than those of the
male. 45 mm.

Caterpillars eat Grasses on bare ground.

We've had to use some difficult words in this book. Here is what they mean.

Brood All the butterflies of one type flying at the same time of year. Many butterflies only have one brood a year, but some have two or three.

Chrysalis Another word for a pupa – the sleepy stage between a caterpillar and a butterfly.

Climate change Our weather is changing because of global warming. Butterflies are very sensitive to weather.

Colony/colonies Groups of a type of butterfly all living and flying together. Many butterflies live in groups, but some live all by themselves.

Common Lots everywhere.

Continent The mainland of Europe, without islands like Britain.

Decline A butterfly that used to be common but isn't any more has declined. Some 75 per cent of British butterflies have declined!

Extinct Gone. In this book, lost from Britain.

Flight season The period when a brood of butterflies is flying.

Food plant A plant (usually the leaves) which the caterpillars of a type of butterfly eat.

Habitat A place that has all the things a butterfly needs – and all the things its eggs, caterpillars and pupae need as well.

Hibernate To sleep through the winter (as a butterfly). Hedgehogs and many other animals also hibernate.

Local Not common or rare. Found only in specific places.

Migrate Lots of birds, like swallows, migrate. They go to a warm country for the winter but fly north to us in summer. Butterflies and birds that do this are called migrants.

Nectar A sweet drink, like honey, inside a flower. Butterflies and bees love it!

Pupa/pupae Also known as a chrysalis. The sleepy stage between a caterpillar and a butterfly. Some pupae live inside a cocoon, which the caterpillar spins out of silk.

Pupate When a caterpillar turns into a pupa (or chrysalis).

Rare A butterfly that only lives in a very few special places, like nature reserves.

Scandinavia The countries of Norway, Sweden and Denmark. Finland, Iceland and the Faroe Islands are also often grouped with the Scandinavian countries.

Species or type Butterflies of the same kind that look the same.

Upper sides and undersides The top and underneath of a butterfly's wings, which usually have different colours and markings.

Veins The 'bones' of a butterfly's wings.

Widespread Colonies dotted around all over the place.

FINDING OUT MORE ABOUT BUTTERFLIES

There are many conservation groups that will help you learn about butterflies. In Britain the big ones are:

County Wildlife Trusts www.wildlifetrusts.org and
their young persons groups, www.wildlifewatch.org
Butterfly Conservation www.butterfly-conservation.org